Making a Difference

RECYCLING
Materials

Sue Barraclough

W
FRANKLIN WATTS
LONDON · SYDNEY

First published in 2006 by
Franklin Watts
338 Euston Road
London NW1 3BH

Franklin Watts Australia
Level 17/207 Kent Street
Sydney NSW 2000

Original concept devised by
Sue Barraclough and Jemima Lumley.

Editor: Adrian Cole
Designer: Jemima Lumley
Art director: Jonathan Hair
Special photography: Mark Simmons (except where listed below)
Consultant: Helen Peake, Education Officer at
  The Recycling Consortium, Bristol

Acknowledgements:
The author and publisher wish to thank Helen Peake and the staff at
The Recycling Consortium. Crystal Paving: 13br, 26br. Green Glass
(www.greenglass.co.uk): 13cl and bl. Paperpod (www.paperpod.co.uk): 27b.
Patagonia (www.patagonia.com): 17br, 26tr. Remarkable Pencils Ltd
(www.remarkable.co.uk): 22 and 26cl. Images on 7c, 7bl, 7br, 9t, 12b, 19b,
25t supplied by the national Recycle Now campaign (for more information
on recycling visit www.recyclenow.com). Chris Fairclough: 15t, 25b.
© Digital Vision: 24. Neil Thomson: 13tl. Bob Daemmrich/Image
Works/Topfoto: 14b. Eastcott-Momatiuk/Topfoto: 19t. David R.
Frazier/Image Works/Topfoto: 11c, 11b. Photri/Topfoto: 16b. Novelis: 15c,
15b. Revolve (www.revolve-uk.com): 27tl.

Special thanks to Connie, James, Romi, Ruby and Vincent for taking part.

A CIP catalogue record for this book is available
from the British Library.

ISBN: 978 0 7496 6483 1
Dewey Classification: 628.4'58

Printed in China

Franklin Watts is a division of Hachette Children's Books,
an Hachette Livre UK company.

Contents

Is it rubbish?

All of these things can be recycled. The materials they are made from can be used again. Recycling helps to save energy and reduce rubbish.

Some materials are used to make the same thing. Other materials are used to make a different object.

Plastic

Paper

None of these things should go into a rubbish bin. They should be recycled.

Glass

Metal

Fruit and vegetable waste

⚠ **Dangerous waste**

Batteries and mobile phones contain dangerous chemicals that need to be specially recycled.

Making compost

Fruit and vegetable waste can be recycled in a compost bin or wormery. The waste changes into compost that can be used to grow more fruit and vegetables.

Plant materials break down naturally. Heat and creatures, such as worms, are part of the process.

Waste in a compost bin becomes mouldy and smelly. The smell means the waste is breaking down. It is changing into something useful.

The plant materials change into compost. It is full of goodness that plants need to grow. People use compost to grow seeds.

Recycling paper

All of these things are made of paper. They can all be recycled.

Printer paper

Junk mail

Magazines

Newspapers

Craft paper

Greetings cards

Wrapping paper

Shredded paper

Paper bags

Waste paper is sorted and chopped up. Then it is cleaned with hot water and mashed up. This changes it into a paper porridge called pulp.

Then the pulp is squeezed and squashed together. It is dried and pressed flat and smooth.

The recycled paper is rolled up and then used to make more paper things.

Recycling glass

These glass bottles and jars can be recycled. Some recycling schemes collect glass from homes. Some people post glass into bottle banks.

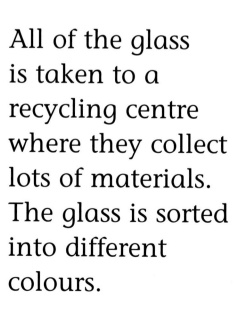

All of the glass is taken to a recycling centre where they collect lots of materials. The glass is sorted into different colours.

Then the glass is crushed, melted and shaped to make new glass bottles and jars.

Different uses for recycled glass

Sometimes the glass is made into other things.

Glass paving

Glass jewellery

Recycling metal

Aluminium and steel are metals used to make drinks cans. Steel is also used to make food tins.

What you can do

Find out if your school has a recycling scheme. You may be able to help sort the recycling.

Recycled metal is sorted, crushed and melted down. The metal can be shaped in lots of ways.

The metal may be used to make more cans. Sometimes it is used to make parts for cars, machines and aeroplanes.

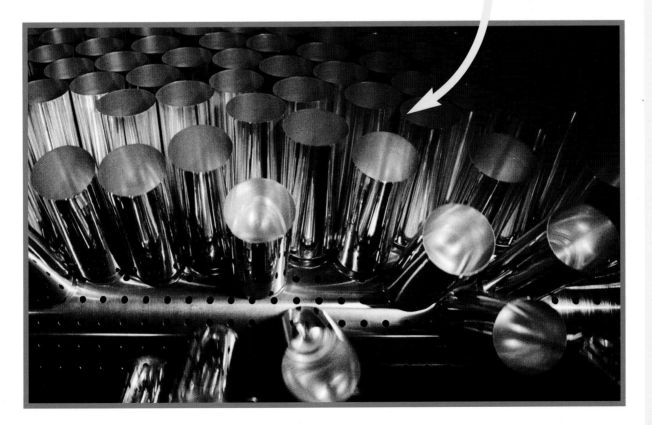

Recycling plastic

There are lots of different kinds of plastic. Most of them are made from oil. Plastic can be thin and flexible, hard and strong, or soft and squashy.

Did you know?

You can take some types of plastic to recycling centres.

Be a plastic spotter!

Look at the number symbols in the triangles. Each one shows what type of plastic the object is made from. There are seven different symbols to spot.

Plastics with the numbers 1 and 2 are most likely to be recycled.

1 PETE
2 HDPE
3 V

4 LDPE
5 PP
6 PS
7 OTHER

Number 1 (PETE or PET) plastic bottles can be recycled to make lots of things. Some are recycled to make fluffy fleeces.

15 bottles will make one fleece.

Ways to recycle

Recycling is simple. Many places have a collection scheme. You leave your materials outside your home in a box. The recyclers come and collect them.

People also take their materials to a special recycling centre. They post each item into a different container.

Sorting recycling

If you know where each material goes, you can sort them easily. Even the youngest members of your family will put things in the right place!

Choose a container to keep your recycling in. Write a label or draw a picture to show everyone what to put in there.

21

Buy recycled

Buying things that are made from recycled materials is very important too.

Pencils

we used to BE plastic cups... (10 pencils)

A mouse mat

I USED TO BE A CAR TYRE...

A notebook

I used to be something else...

A pencil case

I used to be a car tyre...

Pens

WE USED TO BE COMPUTER PRINTERS... (5 pens)

A ruler

I WAS ONCE A COMPUTER PRINTER...

Recycled paper

Did you know?

You can buy toilet paper made from recycled paper. Some playground equipment is made from recycled plastic.

Recycled plastic

Recycle it safely

There are some materials that must be recycled very carefully. Batteries, computers and mobile phones have parts that can be used again.

Dangerous materials are collected and sorted separately. They are taken to special recycling centres.

Old mobile phones and computers have their parts recycled. Some can be repaired and reused.

What you can do

Try not to use normal batteries. Use rechargeable batteries instead.

Batteries contain dangerous chemicals so they need to be specially recycled.

Recycled material?

Can you guess what material has been recycled to make each thing?

1

2

10 pencils

3

4

5

6

Answers on
page 29.

7

Find out more

Ask an adult to call your local council to find out about the services they provide for recycling, or visit their website. They should be able to give you details of their box collection scheme, if they have one, and how to find recycling centres. Try to recycle fewer things by reducing rubbish and reusing things.

www.recyclingglass.co.uk
A website where you can learn about glass recycling.

www.glassforever.co.uk
A user-friendly website packed with facts and information about glass packaging and recycling glass processes.

www.recyclezone.org.uk
Waste Watch website with games, information and activities on recycling, and the 3Rs (Reducing, Reusing and Recycling).

www.collect4school.co.uk
All about recycling at school.

www.thinkcans.com
A website on recycling aluminium cans.

www.recyclemore.co.uk
A great site with lots of information on recycling. It also looks at recycling processes.

www.gould.edu.au/ wastewise
Exciting games, quizzes and other activities to help you learn about recycling.

www.ollierecycles.com/ recycle
News, competitions and information.

Every effort has been made by the Publisher to ensure that these websites contain no inappropriate or offensive material. However, because of the nature of the Internet, it is impossible to guarantee that the contents of these sites will not be altered. We strongly advise that Internet access is supervised by a responsible adult.

Glossary

Bottle bank – a container for storing glass to be recycled.

Compost – plant materials that have broken down. People use compost to help plants grow.

Compost bin – a container used to store kitchen and garden waste where it breaks down to make compost.

Material – the substance something is made from. For example, paper is made from a material called wood.

Recycle – when you use something again or make it into something new.

Recycling collection scheme – a system where materials to be recycled are collected from outside homes.

Wormery – a special container to hold worms and waste. Most kitchen and garden waste, and torn paper and card can be added. It is broken down by the worms.

Answers to the quiz on pages 26–27: 1 – the fleece is made from PET (number 1) plastic bottles; 2 – the outside of the pencils is made from plastic cups; 3 – the paving is made from recycled glass; 4 – the bench is made from recycled plastic; 5 – the mousemat is made from recycled drinks cartons; 6 – the bag is made from rubber from tyre inner tubes; 7– the toy castle is made from recycled paper.

Index

About this book

Making a Difference: Recycling Materials encourages children to help recycle, and to think carefully about the value of materials and how they can be used again. Discuss with children the idea that the world has limited resources, and that if we waste them, they cannot be replaced and may eventually run out.

Explore the idea that it is easy to throw something into a rubbish bin and send it off to a landfill site, but that it is important for us all to realise that if we carry on this way we will run out of space to bury it all.

Page 8 encourages children to see that the rotting process is a natural way to recycle some materials.
Pages 10–17 encourage children to look carefully at materials and to notice similarities and differences. It also helps them to understand the process of recycling.
Page 18 looks at the idea of sorting and storing materials for recycling. Children can play an active part in the process.
Page 22 encourages children to spot recycling symbols in shops.
Pages 24–25 can be used to explore the idea that certain things contain dangerous materials, so they need to be recycled responsibly.
Use **pages 26–27** to promote the idea that we can buy goods made of different recycled materials.